Jamie Mooren
435-8479

Jesus is My Teacher

Learning to read · from the Bible ·

Jesus is My Teacher

By V. Gilbert Beers
Illustrated by Robert Boehmer

ZONDERVAN PUBLISHING HOUSE OF THE ZONDERVAN CORPORATION
GRAND RAPIDS, MICHIGAN 49506

Learning to Read from the Bible Series

GOD IS MY HELPER
GOD IS MY FRIEND
JESUS IS MY TEACHER
JESUS IS MY GUIDE

JESUS IS MY TEACHER
© 1973 by V. GILBERT BEERS
Second Printing—1974
Library of Congress Catalog Card Number 72-95535

Printed in the United States of America

What's in This Book

A Word to Parents and Teachers

Listening to God

Listening to God Tell What He Wants

Exodus 19:16 — 20:18

Listening to God's Word

2 Kings 22; 2 Chronicles 34

Listening to God's Helpers

Acts 8:26-39

Showing Love to Others

Showing God's Love to Others

Luke 10:25-37

A Word to Parents and Teachers

If you could, would you sell your ability to read? How much would you ask for it? Would a few million be enough if you knew that you would never read again? Or is reading one of those assets which are too valuable to give up at any price?

Perhaps you have never thought of reading skills in terms of dollars and cents. If you have, you realize how precious they are. You realize also how important it is for your children to develop the best reading skills possible.

What, then, would you give to see your children reading to the best of their abilities? And what would you give to see them have the best available reading materials?

Fortunately, most of us today are heirs to a good reading program through public or private schools. Some of us inherit a better program than others. But parents and teachers would likely agree that most children are learning to read better and faster than they learned a generation ago.

Reading materials are superior today, too. There are hundreds of good books for children, filled with beautiful pictures. But for some reason, Christian reading materials have not kept pace with general reading materials. There are few colorful books about the Bible at the beginning reader level.

This book has been developed to help fill that need. It is for the child who has reached the basic reading level, wherever he may be — at school, home, or Sunday school.

But this book is more than a Bible reader. It includes more than a basic knowledge of what the Bible says. Questions which follow each Bible story help the reader relate that story to his own life. They help him understand how his life fits into God's plans and how God's plans fit into his life.

A section after each story called "New Things for Me to Do" helps the reader discover simple ways to put the Bible truths he has learned into his everyday experiences.

You may be a parent who is looking for a devotional book which your child can read himself. Or you may be a teacher who is seeking some supplementary reading material for your pupils. Or perhaps you are a Sunday school teacher who would like some additional reading material for class or home use. It is our prayer that this book will meet these needs — and more.

V. Gilbert Beers

Listening
to
God

Listening to God
Tell What He Wants

"Thunder!" some people said.

"Lightning!" said others.

Moses' people were afraid of the thunder. They were afraid of the lightning over the mountain.

Moses' people were afraid of the things they saw.

Then the people heard another sound. It was very loud.

"What is that?" some of them asked.

"It is like a trumpet," said others. "But it is so loud."

The people were even more afraid now. They had never heard a sound like that before.

"Come with me," Moses told his people. "Come near the mountain. God will talk to me there."

The people walked behind Moses. They went near the big mountain.

Suddenly, big clouds went up from the mountain. The trumpet sound became louder and louder. Then God began to talk to Moses. When God talked, His words sounded like more thunder.

Moses went up on the mountain to hear what God would say. God had told him to do this. Moses listened to God.

"You must go down again to your people," God told Moses. "You must tell them not to walk on this mountain. If they do, they will die."

So Moses went down to his people. He told them what God had said. The people listened to the things God had said. They did not walk on the mountain.

When Moses went down to his people, he told them what God had said.

Where can you learn more about God?

Moses went up on the mountain again. Then God told him what He wanted the people to do. This is what God said.

Do not love anything else more than Me.

Do not make anything that you will want more than Me.

Do not say My name in a bad way.

On My day, do things that please Me.

Love your mother and father.

Do not kill people.

Do not do things that hurt people you love.

Do not take things that are not yours.

Do not say things that are not true.

Do not want things you cannot have.

New Words I Have Learned

thunder	Moses	trumpet
lightning	God	listen
	Bible	

New Thoughts to Think About

1. Did Moses and his people read the Bible? No, they did not have a Bible. Then how did they know what God wanted?

2. How do you know what God wants? Do you have a Bible?

3. Do you listen to the things God says in the Bible? Do you try to do them each day?

New Things for Me to Do

Where can we learn more about God? Read the words on the boy's wall. Talk with someone about other ways to learn what God wants.

The people were glad to see what King Josiah did.

Listening to God's Word

"Josiah is our new king," the people shouted.

The people were very happy. They were glad to have a new king.

"But our new king is only a boy," some people said. "Can a boy be a good king?"

When King Josiah became older, the people were glad to see what he did.

"Take down those altars," Josiah shouted. "My people must not worship other gods at those altars. They must worship our God."

King Josiah watched his men take down the altars. He wanted to know that it was done.

"Beat those things into little pieces," said the new king.

Josiah loved God. He wanted his people to love God, too.

"We will put God's house together again," said the king. "We will make God's house beautiful."

Once God's house had been very beautiful. But some kings before Josiah did not take care of it. They did not love God. So they did not take care of His house.

The people were glad to help the king. They were glad to help make God's house beautiful again.

"We must read God's Word to all the people," said the king. So he did.

One day a man found something in God's house. "Look! Look!" he shouted. "Here is part of God's Word!"

"Read it to me," said King Josiah.

The man read God's Word to the king. The king listened to the things God said.

"We have not been doing what God wants," the king said. "We must read this to all the people."

So the king had all of the people listen to God's Word. He had it read in God's house.

"God is telling us what He wants," said the king. "I will do what He says. I want you to do what He says, too."

The people were happy to do what God said. They were happy, too, that their king listened to God.

Talk about some places where God's Word is read today.

New Words I Have Learned

Josiah   altar   worship

piece   teacher

New Thoughts to Think About

1. What did King Josiah do to show that he loved God? Do you listen to God's Word? Do you help to make God's house beautiful?

2. What should we do when we hear God's Word? Do you try to do what God says in His Word?

New Things for Me to Do

King Josiah's people did not have all of the Bible. They had only one part of it. And they had only one to read. So someone had to read it to the others at God's house.

But you have your own Bible. You can take it anywhere. Talk with Mother or Father or your teacher. Talk about some places where God's Word is read today. Then thank God for giving you all of His Word.

Listening to God's Helpers

"You must go away from here," an angel said to Philip. "You must go where I tell you."

"Go away from here?" Philip thought. "But I am doing God's work here. I am helping many people know about God. Why should I go away?"

Philip called to the man in the chariot.

"Because God wants you in another place," said the angel. "It is a road far away from here."

Philip knew that he must do what God wanted. He must go away. He must go to a new place where God wanted him.

So Philip went with the angel. He went away to another place. It was a road far from the city.

"How can I work for God here?" Philip thought. "There are no people. There is no one to listen when I tell about Jesus."

Suddenly, Philip saw a chariot on the road. He saw a man riding in the chariot.

"Go and talk to that man," God told Philip.

Philip ran to the chariot. He called to the man in the chariot.

The man in the chariot was going home to

Philip told the man what God said in His Word.

Africa. He was reading something as he rode in the chariot. It was God's Word.

"Do you know what that says?" Philip asked the man.

"No," said the man. "I need someone to help me."

The man stopped the chariot. He asked

Philip to ride with him. Philip told him what God said in His Word. He told the man about Jesus.

"I want to love Jesus and follow Him," said the man. "I want to be His helper."

Now Philip knew why God told him to come here. This man would tell many other people in Africa about Jesus.

Philip was so glad that he had listened to God's angel. And he was glad that this man in the chariot had listened to God's Word.

How many of God's helpers can you find in this picture?

New Words I Have Learned

angel	Philip	chariot
Africa	Jesus	picture

New Thoughts to Think About

1. Why did God send Philip to a new place? Why did He take Philip away from His work?

2. God takes some things from us so He can give us something better. Has God ever done this to you?

3. Can we do what God wants if we do not listen to Him? Why should you listen to God's helpers?

New Things for Me to Do

Look at the picture. Who do you see? How many of God's helpers can you find? God's helpers are people or things that help us know about God. Are you one of God's helpers? Do you help others know more about God?

Showing
Love
to
Others

"What must I do to live with God?" a man asked Jesus. "How can I live always in His house some day?"

"What does God tell you?" Jesus asked. "What does He say in His Word?"

The man thought about this. He knew many things about God's Word.

"God says we must love Him very much," the man said. "We must show His love to others. We must be good neighbors."

"Then you should do this," Jesus told the man.

"But who is a good neighbor?" the man asked. "How can I be a good neighbor?"

Jesus told the man a story. In Jesus' story, this is what happened.

Which man was a good neighbor?

One day a man walked along a road. Suddenly some bad men hit him and hurt him. They took his money. Then they ran away and left him.

Soon a man came down the road. He told people that he was God's helper. But he did not stop to help this man.

Then another man came along the road. He also told people that he was God's helper. But he did not stop to help the man who was hurt.

Later, another man came by. He did not tell people that he was God's helper. He was a Samaritan. The man who was hurt was a Jew. The Jews did not like the Samaritans. But the Samaritan loved God. So he loved the man who was hurt. He stopped to help him.

"Which man was a good neighbor?" Jesus asked.

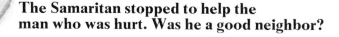

The Samaritan stopped to help the man who was hurt. Was he a good neighbor?

Tell some person about Jesus.
Tell him how much he needs Jesus.

The man thought about this. He knew what Jesus was saying.

"The man who *was* God's helper," he said. "Not the men who *said* they were God's helpers."

"That is what God wants you to do," said Jesus. "Love God. Be His helper. Show His love to others."

The man went away from Jesus. He wanted to tell people that he was God's helper. But he did not want to show God's love to others.

New Words I Have Learned

neighbor   story   person

Samaritan   Jew

New Thoughts to Think About

1. Are you a good neighbor? Do you show God's love to others? Or do you just *say* that you are God's helper?

2. Jesus told how to please God. He knows what God wants. That is because He is God's Son. Ask Jesus to help you please God more.

New Things for Me to Do

Think of some person who does not know God. Do you think God loves him? Do you love him? Then tell him about Jesus. Tell him how much he needs Jesus. Show him that you love God by telling him about God's love.

"Will you help me do some work today?"
a man asked his boy.

Showing God's Love
by Doing What God Wants

One day Jesus told a story. This is what He said.

"Will you help me do some work today?" a man asked his boy.

"No," said the boy. "I want to do something else."

The father was sad when he heard that. But he had another boy. He would ask him to help.

"Will you help me do some work today?" he asked.

"Yes," said the other boy. "I will help you."

The father was happy when he heard that. He went to get some things so they could work.

While the father was gone, the two boys began to think. The first boy was sad because he had said no. The second boy was sad because he had said yes.

"I will stay here and help my father," said the first boy.

"I will run away and have fun," said the second boy.

When the father came back, he saw the first boy.

"I am sorry that I said no," said the first boy. "I will help you."

"Good," said the father. "But where is your brother?"

"He ran away to have fun," said the first boy.

When Jesus was through telling the story, He talked with some people. These people were called Pharisees. They said they loved God. But they did not do God's work.

"Which boy did what his father wanted?" Jesus asked.

"The first boy," the Pharisees said.

"Yes. But you are like the second boy," said Jesus. "You told God you would work for Him. But you do not. Some other people said they would not work for God. You thought they were bad people. But they asked God for a new life. Now they work for Him."

The Pharisees did not like what Jesus said. But they knew that He was right. It is better to *do* God's work than to *say* you will do it.

Do one of these for God each day.

New Words I Have Learned

second   sorry   brother

Pharisees

New Thoughts to Think About

1. Did the Pharisees do God's work? Or did they just say they would do it?

2. Do you do God's work? Or do you just say you will do it?

New Things for Me to Do

What are some things you can do for God? What kind of work does He want you to do? Talk with Mother or Father or your teacher. Cut out some numbers. Put one of these on each number. Then do one for God each day.

Talk to God.

Read about God.

Tell someone about Jesus.

Showing Love
When We Could Get Hurt

"Please," the boy said, "may I talk to my Uncle Paul?"

"Yes," said the soldiers. "You may go in. You may talk to him."

The boy's Uncle Paul was in jail. Some people did not like him. They did not like the good

The soldiers let the boy talk to his Uncle Paul.

things he said about Jesus. They had helped to kill Jesus. So these people had Paul put into jail.

"Now they want to kill you," the boy said to his uncle. "I heard some of them. They will kill you when the soldiers take you out."

"You are very brave to come here," said Paul. "Those men would kill you if they could. But you should tell the captain what you told me."

The captain was the man who led the soldiers. He would not want Paul to be killed. He listened

That night, the soldiers took Paul to another city.

to the boy. Then he thought about the things the boy said.

"Do not tell anyone else," he said. "I will help your uncle."

When the boy left, the captain talked to some soldiers. He told the soldiers what they must do.

"Get some horses," he said. "We will take Paul to another city. We will go when it is night."

The soldiers did what the captain said. They

Put some big letters on your wall.

got some horses. They got other soldiers to help them.

That night the soldiers left the city. The captain led them to another city. They took Paul with them.

The bad men could not kill Paul now. Paul could tell many more people about Jesus.

Paul was glad that the boy loved him. The boy had helped him, even when he could have been hurt.

New Words I Have Learned

Paul   soldiers   jail

          captain

New Thoughts to Think About

1. How could the boy have been hurt? Do you think he loved his Uncle Paul? What did he do to show his love?

2. Think of some people you love. Do you love your mother and father? Do you love God? Do you show your love for them? How? Do you show your love even when you could get hurt?

New Things for Me to Do

Cut some big letters **L O V E** from paper. Write one of these on each letter. Put them on your wall. They will tell you how you could get hurt by showing love.

 Friends may make fun of me.

 Someone may not thank me.

 Someone may do something to me.

 I may have to give up some money.

Talking
With
God

The boy and his father saw some people. Then they saw Jesus.

Jesus Tells Us
How to Talk to God

"Where are we going?" a boy asked his father.

His father smiled. "We are going to hear Jesus," he said. "Jesus will talk to us today."

"But why are we going up this mountain?" the boy asked.

"Jesus wants to talk to His friends now," said the father. "He does not want other people to listen. So we must go up on the mountain. We can be with Jesus there."

The boy and his father walked for a long time. At last they saw some other people. Then they saw Jesus.

The people listened to Jesus. They wanted to hear what He said.

Jesus told them many things. He told them how to be happy. He told them how to please God. Then Jesus told the people how to pray.

"This is the way you should pray," Jesus said.

The people listened to the things Jesus said.

Our Father, You live in heaven.
Let us think good things about Your name.
Please be our King as soon as You can.

Help us to please You here,

as the angels do in heaven.

Help us to get food to eat each day.

Forgive the bad things we do.

Help us to forgive others who hurt us.

Keep us from thinking about bad things.

Keep us from doing bad things.

You are the One who should lead us.

You are the One who can help us.

For You are greater than anyone else.

These words will tell you what you can say to God.

New Words I Have Learned

pray   heaven   forgive

                        great

New Thoughts to Think About

1. Who do we talk to when we pray? Does God want you to talk to Him? Why?
2. Do you pray each day? What do you say to God?

New Things for Me to Do

Ask Mother or Father to help you write some words on a piece of paper. Put them on your window. Here are some words to write. They will tell you what you can say when you pray.

ASK — You can ask God for things.

THANK — You can thank God for things.

HAPPY — You can tell God you are happy.

LOVE — You can tell God you love Him.

Look at the words each day. They will help you to pray better.

Jesus Talks to God

"Come with Me," Jesus said to His friends.
Jesus and His friends had been eating supper
together. Now they were through. It was time
to go.

Jesus and His friends went out to the street.
It was night now. Most of the people were
in their houses. The animals had gone to sleep.

Jesus and His friends walked quietly through
the city. They stopped at a garden. The garden

Jesus and His friends walked
quietly through the city.

was on a big hill. It had many trees. The garden was called Gethsemane.

"You will run away from Me," Jesus said to His friends. "You will run away before it is morning."

"No, we will not run away from You," said Peter. He was one of Jesus' friends. Peter loved Jesus very much.

"Peter, you will even tell people you do not know Me," said Jesus.

Peter and his friends were sad when they heard that. What would happen that night? Why would they run away from Jesus?

Then Jesus began to pray. He talked to God about the things that would happen. Jesus knew that some bad men would take Him. Then they would kill Him.

"Father, is there some other way to do what

You want to do?" Jesus prayed. "If there is, do not let this happen to Me."

Then Jesus told God something we must tell Him, too. "But do what You want to do," He said. "Not what I want to do."

Jesus went back to talk to some of His friends. But they were sleeping.

"Must you sleep now?" Jesus asked.

Jesus talked to God about the things that would happen.

Look at this question each time you go out of your room.

Jesus' friends were sad when He said that. They knew they should be praying. But they were very tired. So they went to sleep again when Jesus went away to pray.

At last some bad men came to the garden. They took Jesus away to kill Him.

Jesus was ready to do what God wanted because He had prayed. But His friends had been sleeping. They were not ready to do what God wanted. So they ran away.

New Words I Have Learned

Peter	Gethsemane	supper
question	tired	answer

New Thoughts to Think About

1. Are you ready to do what God wants? You will be more ready when you pray.
2. Was Jesus ready to do what God wanted? Why? Were Jesus' friends ready? Why not?

New Things for Me to Do

Write this question on some big paper. Put it over the door of your room. Look at it each time you go out of your door.

Am I ready to do what God wants?

If you answer no, go back in your room and pray.

Jesus' friends went upstairs to
a big room in a house.

Jesus' Friends Talk to God

"Jesus is gone," His friends said. "He has gone to live in Heaven again."

"But what should we do now?" some of them asked.

Jesus' friends were called disciples. They had followed Jesus. But they did not know what to do now.

Jesus had told His disciples to go into the city. He had told them to wait for something.

But the disciples did not know what they were waiting for. And they did not know what to do while they waited.

So Jesus' friends went into the city. They went to a big room in a house. The room was upstairs.

"What should we do now?" some of them asked again.

Jesus' friends prayed in the room each day.

"I know," said one disciple. "We should pray. We should talk to God while we are waiting."

"Yes," said the others. "That is a good thing to do."

One by one, Jesus' friends prayed. They

talked to God about many things. They asked
Him to help them.

As Jesus' disciples prayed, they began to
think about Jesus. They began to think about
each other, too.

Jesus' friends came to that room each day.
They kept on praying. They asked God to
show them what to do about many things.

God was with them in the room. He showed them the right way to do His work. He helped them love each other more. He helped them know what He wanted.

Jesus' disciples learned many good things. While we wait for God to help us, we should talk to God. Then we will learn many good things about God, too.

Which boy and girl are doing the best thing?

New Words I Have Learned

upstairs   disciple

New Thoughts to Think About

1. What did Jesus' friends do while they waited? Was that a good thing to do?

2. Are you waiting for something? What are you doing while you wait? What should you do?

New Things for Me to Do

Look at the pictures of the boys and girls. They are all waiting for something great to happen. Which boy and girl are doing the best thing while they wait?

Forgiving
Others

"Go to Egypt and buy food," Jaco[b] told his sons.

Joseph Forgives His Brothers

"I want something to eat," a boy said.

"We all want something to eat," Grandfather Jacob said. "But there is not much food to eat."

No one in Jacob's country had much food. Only the people in Egypt had food. They had more food than they needed. So they began to sell some.

"Go to Egypt and buy food," Jacob told his sons.

Jacob's sons did not want to go to Egypt. Many years before, they had a brother named Joseph. They hated Joseph. So they sold him. He had been taken to Egypt to be a slave. What if they saw Joseph there?

"But we must go," said some of them. "We must get food to eat. And we can not tell our father what we did to Joseph."

So Jacob's sons went to Egypt. They bought food from the governor. But the governor made one of them stay in Egypt. Then he let the others go home with the food.

When the food was gone, Jacob's sons went back to Egypt. They went to get more food.

Jacob's sons went to see the governor again. "We want to buy some food," they said.

"First, you must eat with me," said the governor.

Jacob's sons were surprised. Why would the governor eat with them?

The next day, the governor made Jacob's sons come back. They were afraid now. Why did the governor do this?

"Please do not hurt us," they said.

"I will not hurt you," said the governor. "I am your brother, Joseph!"

The brothers were so surprised! Joseph was not a slave. He was governor of all Egypt.

The brothers were so surprised that the governor was Joseph.

Do you forgive others when they are sorry?

Joseph knew that his brothers were sorry. They were sorry that they had sold him.

"I forgive you," said Joseph. "Please bring my father here. Then you must come and live here, too. I will take care of you."

The brothers were very happy. How good it was to have a brother like Joseph!

New Words I Have Learned

Joseph	grandfather	Jacob
Egypt	slave	bought
	governor	

New Thoughts to Think About

1. What do people do when they forgive? Did Joseph forgive his brothers? Why did he do this? What had they done to him?

2. Has someone done something bad to you? Is he sorry? Do you forgive him? Can you ask God to forgive you if you do not forgive others?

New Things for Me to Do

Some words are missing here. Can you tell what they are?

Joseph _____ his brothers.

So, he _____ them.

loved   hated

killed   forgave

A Servant Does Not Forgive

One day Jesus told His disciples a story. This is the story that Jesus told.

There was a king who had much money. He had many servants. The king let some of the servants use his money.

But the king found that one servant had taken too much money. The king knew that the servant could not pay it all back.

"How much can you pay me?" the king asked.

The servant asked the king to
be kind to him.

"I will put you in jail," shouted the first servant.

"I have no money now," said the servant. "So I can not pay you anything."

"You do not have any of that money?" the king said. "Then I will put you in jail. I will sell your wife and children."

"Please do not do that," the servant said. He got down on his knees. He asked the king to be kind to him.

The king felt sorry for the servant. He did not want to put him in jail. He did not want to sell his wife and children.

"You do not have to give back the money," the king said. "I will not put you in jail. I will not sell your wife and children."

"Thank you! Thank you!" said the servant. Then he went out.

On his way home, the servant saw another servant. This man had to pay the first servant some money. But he did not have the money.

"I will put you in jail," shouted the first servant. "I will sell your wife and children."

"Please don't do that," the other servant begged.

But the first servant was not kind. He put the other servant in jail. He sold his wife and children.

The king was very angry when he heard that. He made the first servant come to see him again.

"You are a very bad man," the king shouted.

"I was kind to you. But you were not kind to the other servant."

The man begged the king to be kind again. But the king was too angry.

"Put him in jail," the king said. "Do not let him out until he pays me all the money."

When Jesus had told the story, He talked to His disciples. "God wants you to forgive others," He said. "If you do not, God will not forgive you."

Should we keep on talking about someone when we forgive them?

New Words I Have Learned

servant wife knee

felt sin begged

New Thoughts to Think About

1. Should we ask God to forgive us when we do something bad? Does God want to forgive us?

2. Should God forgive us if we do not forgive others? What should we do first then?

New Things for Me to Do

Which of these should we do when we forgive someone?

1. Keep talking about his sin
2. Stop talking about his sin
3. Keep thinking about his sin
4. Stop thinking about his sin
5. Keep on being angry about his sin
6. Stop being angry about his sin

The soldiers nailed Jesus to a cross.

Jesus Forgives
Some Men Who Hurt Him

"Take that Man over there!"

"Nail His hands and feet to that cross!"

The soldiers hurried to do what their leader told them. They took Jesus to a cross. They nailed His hands and feet to it.

Jesus did not say anything. He was very quiet.

Jesus had never hurt these men. But they were hurting Him.

The soldiers had to hurt Jesus. They had been told to do it.

Jesus felt sorry for the soldiers. They had to do what they were told. They had to hurt a Man they did not know.

Suddenly Jesus said something. The soldiers listened. They wanted to hear what this Man said.

"Father, forgive them," said Jesus. "They do not know what they are doing."

The soldiers looked at each other. This Man did not say mean things to them. He did not say mean things about them. He asked God to forgive them.

That day, the soldiers watched Jesus on the cross. They watched Him die. They had

"That Man is God's Son," said the leader of the soldiers.

Write the words so they will tell you something about forgiving.

never seen anyone like Jesus. Jesus forgave the people who hurt Him.

"That Man is God's Son," said the leader of the soldiers.

Nobody knows what the other soldiers thought. But they must have thought that He was God's Son, too. Only God's Son could forgive them like that!

New Words I Have Learned

nail   cross   leader

mean   nobody   forgave

New Thoughts to Think About

1. Do most people forgive the way Jesus did? What do most of us do when people hurt us?

2. Why do you think Jesus forgave the soldiers? Did He want to see them hurt?

3. Do you forgive people who try to hurt you? Should you? Jesus' people should.

New Things for Me to Do

These words will tell you something about forgiving. But you must put them together in the right way. Write them on some paper. Can you do that?

forgive   I   as   me   must

others   Jesus   forgives

What These Stories Teach

Each story in this book teaches an important Bible truth, or doctrine. Each story also teaches an important truth about the child's daily living.

These two truths, or objectives, are often so closely related within a story that they may not be obvious to the parent or teacher. All objectives, doctrinal and present-day, are listed here so they may be clearly understood by the parent or teacher.

Story	Doctrinal objectives	Present-day objectives
Listening to God Tell What He Wants	The Bible tells us what God wants us to do.	We should read the Bible each day to learn God's will.
Listening to God's Word	The Bible is God's Word for all people.	We should thank God that we have His Word and try to understand it.
Listening to God's Helpers	God uses some people to be His helpers.	We should listen to God's helpers for they can teach us much about Him.
Showing God's Love to Others	Those who love God should show His love to others.	We should tell others about God's love and show that His love has changed us.
Showing God's Love by Doing What God Wants	God wants His people to *do* His work instead of just *talk* about it.	We should look for ways to do what God wants and not merely talk about it.

Showing Love When We Could Get Hurt	When we really love people, we should be willing to help them, even when it may cost us something.	We should look for ways to help those we love and those God loves.
Jesus Tells Us How to Talk to God	God wants us to talk to Him.	We can tell God many things.
Jesus Talks to God	Praying gets us ready to do what God wants.	We should pray much to help us prepare to do what God wants.
Jesus' Friends Talk to God	God wants us to talk to Him while we wait for something important.	We should pray for God's help while we wait for God's will.
Joseph Forgives His Brothers	God wants us to forgive others, even if they have hurt us.	We should forgive others when they are sorry.
A Servant Does Not Forgive	God will forgive us when we have forgiven others.	We must forgive others before we ask God to forgive us.
Jesus Forgives Some Men Who Hurt Him	Jesus forgave people who hurt Him.	We must forgive others the way Jesus did.

Basic Word List

Most of the 287 words on this basic list will be familiar to your child. These words have come primarily from standard word lists used in public-school education, and include some of the most frequently used words in basic reading textbooks.

With each Bible story, you will find a list of new words which are not found in this list. Later, a cumulative list of all new words is given.

Variants of a word are usually not considered new words in this book. These include words made by adding s, es, ies, ing, ed, er, est, iest, or ly. Thus, talks, talked, and talking are not considered new words since talk is on the basic word list.

a	beat	clothes
about	beautiful	cloud
afraid	became	come
again	because	could
all	been	country
along	before	cut
also	began	day
always	behind	did
am	best	die
an	better	do
and	big	does
angry	book	done
animal	boy	door
another	brave	down
anyone	bring	each
anything	but	eat
anywhere	buy	else
are	by	even
as	call	ever
ask	came	far
at	can	father
away	cannot	feet
back	care	find
bad	children	first
be	city	

u	*s*	*b*
follow	into	mountain
food	is	much
for	it	must
found	just	my
friend	keep	name
from	kill	near
fun	kind	need
garden	king	never
get	knew	new
girl	know	next
give	last	night
glad	late	no
go	lead	not
gone	learn	now
good	led	number
had	left	of
hand	let	off
happen	letter	old
happy	life	on
has	like	once
hate	little	one
have	live	only
he	long	or
hear	look	other
heard	loud	our
help	love	out
here	made	over
hill	make	own
him	man	paper
his	many	part
hit	may	pay
home	me	people
horse	mean	place
house	men	please
how	money	put
hurry	more	quiet
hurt	morning	ran
I	most	read
if	mother	ready
in		

ride	take	us
right	talk	use
road	tell	very
room	than	wait
run	thank	walk
sad	that	wall
said	the	want
saw	their	was
say	them	watch
see	then	way
sell	there	we
send	these	went
should	they	were
shout	thing	what
show	think	when
sit	this	where
sleep	those	which
smile	thought	while
so	through	who
sold	time	why
some	to	will
someone	today	window
something	together	with
son	told	word
soon	too	work
sound	took	would
stay	tree	write
stop	true	year
street	try	yes
sudden	two	you
surprise	uncle	your
	until	
	up	

New Word List

In each story throughout this volume, new words are shown in the section "New Words I Have Learned." New words are those included in that story, but not included in the basic word list.

The following is a cumulative list of those sixty-two new words used in the child's reading material. Words used in the instructions to parents and teachers are not considered for either of these lists.

No more than seven new words are used with each Bible story. Sometimes a smaller number is used.

Because these are Bible stories, many of the words are "specialized vocabulary words" relating to the Bible. These specialized Bible words will help to acquaint your beginning reader with Bible names and terms which he should begin to know.

Africa
altar
angel
answer
begged
Bible
bought
brother
captain
chariot
cross
disciple
Egypt
felt
forgave
forgive
Gethsemane
God
governor
grandfather

great
heaven
Jacob
jail
Jesus
Jew
Joseph
Josiah
knee
leader
lightning
listen
mean
Moses
nail
neighbor
nobody
Paul
person
Peter
Pharisees
Philip

picture
piece
pray
question
Samaritan
second
servant
sin
slave
soldiers
sorry
story
supper
teacher
thunder
tired
trumpet
upstairs
wife
worship